JESUS
HANDS
AND OURS

JESUS'
HANDS
AND OURS

Tony Kidd

Scripture Union

Scripture Union, 207–209 Queensway, Bletchley, MK2 2EB, England.
Email: info@scriptureunion.org.uk
Web site: www.scriptureunion.org.uk

British Library Cataloguing-in-Publication Data
A catalogue record for this book is available from the British Library.

Cover design by Grax Design.
Illustrations by Helen Gale.
Printed and bound in Great Britain by Creative Print and Design (Wales),
Ebbw Vale.

SCRIPTURE UNION

We are an international Christian charity working with churches in more
than 130 countries providing resources to bring the good news about
Jesus Christ to children, young people and families – and to encourage
them to develop spiritually through the Bible and prayer.

As well as our network of volunteers, staff and associates who run
holidays, church-based events and school Christian groups, we produce a
wide range of publications and support those who use our resources
through training programmes.

CONTENTS

PREFACE

Those who seek to control others, or to entrench their own positions (or both!), very frequently turn to language in order to achieve their objectives. By the skilful manipulation of words, the propagandist or spin doctor can dominate the media, control public opinion, influence events, or belittle and exclude those who don't fit into their view of the world. Either people have to 'join our club' and 'sing from the same hymn-sheet', or they are left behind, rendered powerless or voiceless. And these manipulators of words can do serious damage, unleashing destructive forces leaving people's lives, relationships, families, even whole societies in ruins.

Jesus of Nazareth recognised all too well the danger of abusing power through language. We may take as an example the way he challenged the Pharisees (Matthew 23:1–24), taking them to task for their approach to the law. That was because they used their views on compliance with the law as a means of control. Jesus, on the other hand, saw the law in terms of values that are eternally and universally applicable. What he said in effect was that the law by itself is useless if we do not also live it out in our hearts and in our lives. Obviously, we cannot do this through the sometimes arrogant and arbitrary manipulation of language.

The Pharisees used language as a tool for maintaining their grip on the levers of power. Propagandists who call terrorists 'freedom fighters', political spin doctors who cloak lies in the garb of truth, power-brokers who use the media to propagate their brand of reality, do the same in our own time. In stark contrast, Jesus took hold of language and brought it to life, giving his words force and meaning by his very actions, and applying them creatively within his own life and work. Supremely, he took the words of the law and drew forth from them words of love: we see this love played out in his death and resurrection.

The sessions in this course are designed to help us see love in action through the hands of Jesus in a way that is both understandable and accessible to ordinary people. It is my hope that you will also be encouraged to imitate Jesus' loving actions in your daily life.

INTRODUCTION

If, as has been suggested, the eye is the window of the soul, then perhaps the hand is its practical means of expression. As we direct the actions of our hands we give effect to our thoughts and attitudes, however deep or shallow these may be. The hand proffered in friendship carries no weapon, but the hand clutching a missile obviously constitutes a threat. 'You cannot shake hands with a clenched fist' (Indira Gandhi).

For those who profess Jesus of Nazareth as Lord, his example is both instructive and challenging. Throughout his ministry, he took up no weapons to defend either himself or his followers; yet in the end he triumphed over his enemies even though they nailed him to a cross. Yet for each and every example that Jesus gives of using his hands and their actions to bring comfort, be creative or make sacrifices, there is an opposite. It seems all too easy in today's world to be disruptive, destructive and grasping.

This course tries to help its participants discover how they can be positive and compassionate as well as obedient to the example we have been given in Jesus. It has been written primarily for use by groups, although it may also be helpful to individuals. A group of six to ten people is ideal. Group members may like to appoint a leader, or take it in turns over the six weeks to be responsible for facilitating the group and keeping time. Allow between one-and-a-half and two hours for each session. Suggested timings for the specific sections are as follows:

Way in....... 10–15 minutes   Response... 15–20 minutes
Bible.......... 20–30 minutes   Prayer .... 10–20 minutes
Life............ 5–10 minutes   *includ – Music*

Included are suggestions for songs which reflect the theme for each session and these can be found in Mission Praise (MP), Songs of Fellowship (SOF) and The Source (TS). There are also suggestions for music to be played when leading into times of prayer or during the meditations.

The Bible passages are from New Revised Standard Version (NRSV) and are printed in full. The group may prefer to read these in silence. Alternatively:
- One person reads the passage aloud while the others listen.
- Two or three people read alternate verses.
- One person takes the role of narrator while others read any dialogue.

The meditations may be approached in three ways:
- You may like to read them on your own silently or, if no one else is near, out loud.
- If you are in a group, one person might read the meditation to the others. The passage should be read slowly, with pauses at appropriate points to allow time for people to take in the atmosphere and bring their imaginations into play.
- If the person reading to the group is feeling fairly confident, they might use the meditation as a basis for painting their own picture of the scene, pausing after each line to inject imagery or description.

An illustration appears near each meditation to provide a focus, but you may like to bring an appropriate object such as a spray of leaves or flowers, a cross or a candle. Other pictures, either photographs or prints of paintings, can be used. Be creative in thinking up ways to add interest and variety.

NOTE

At times of sharing, no one should feel obliged to say more than they want to, and individual privacy must always be respected. As a group, be sensitive to the possibility that some members may find parts of the sessions difficult. Providing support in such circumstances could be helpful. The text contains points at which silence can be used.

Some may find silence uncomfortable, so offer reassurance beforehand. Let people know how long the silence will last, and that they can use it for quiet prayer, to unburden themselves from the pressures of the day, or simply to be still before God.

The pattern of prayer on pages 19–21 is designed for use each day during the course, and may be adapted to suit personal taste and practice. The daily readings form a natural part of the pattern of prayer. The following are the readings for the three days before the first meeting:

Preparation	Day 1	Deuteronomy 28:8–12; Hands blessed in their work
	Day 2	Isaiah 45:7–12; Hands that created the heavens
	Day 3	1 Thessalonians 4:1–2,9–12; 5:12–23; The daily work of the believer
◆ Meeting	Day 4	John 6:5–13; Hands that created much out of little

1 HANDS THAT CREATED

Aim: To look at the part that creativity plays in our lives.

WAY IN 10 - 15 mi.

Spend a few minutes with another member of the group talking about the part that being creative plays in your life. Pray with each other about anything that either of you wishes to bring before God. *Remember prayers for later*

Songs to sing
Change my heart, O God, SOF 58, MP 69, TS 68.
Come to the waters, MP 104.
I lift my hands, SOF 222, MP 280.
In moments like these, SOF 241, MP 334, TS 229.
Jesus, You are changing me, SOF 311, MP 389.
Lord, make me an instrument, SOF 360, MP 437.—
How great Thou art, SOF 425, MP 506, TS 396.
Rejoice, rejoice! SOF 480, MP 572, TS 438.
Rock of ages, SOF 488, MP 582.
What a friend we have in Jesus, SOF 593, MP 746, TS 566.

Music to listen to
Yo-Yo Ma: '*Gigue from Suite No. 4 in E flat major*', from Bach:

The Six Unaccompanied Cello Suites.
Ladysmith Black Mambazo: *'Lungisa Indela Yakho'* ('The path is clear') from In Harmony.
Libera: *'Dies Irae'*, from Libera. — Daring worship

use — pg. 11 also

20 - 30

John 6:5–13

[5] When he looked up and saw a large crowd coming towards him, Jesus said to Philip, 'Where are we to buy bread for these people to eat?' [6] He said this to test him, for he himself knew what he was going to do. [7] Philip answered him, 'Six months' wages would not buy enough bread for each of them to get a little.' [8] One of his disciples, Andrew, Simon Peter's brother, said to him, [9] 'There is a boy here who has five barley loaves and two fish. But what are they among so many people?' [10] Jesus said, 'Make the people sit down.' Now there was a great deal of grass in the place; so they sat down, about five thousand in all. [11] Then Jesus took the loaves, and when he had given thanks, he distributed them to those who were seated; so also the fish, as much as they wanted. [12] When they were satisfied, he told his disciples, 'Gather up the fragments left over, so that nothing may be lost.' [13] So they gathered them up, and from the fragments of the five barley loaves, left by those who had eaten, they filled twelve baskets.

'Isn't this the carpenter's son?', asked the people of Jesus' home town as they puzzled over the source of his wisdom and miraculous powers (Matthew 13:54–55). This was after the many instances of healing and miracles that occurred at the beginning of his ministry.

In the miracle of the feeding of the five thousand, Jesus employed his hands to create something out of almost nothing, using the five loaves and two fish to demonstrate his power to feed the many people who had flocked to hear him. In giving thanks and distributing the loaves and the fish, Jesus used his hands to give expression to the same creative process that brought light and life out of a dark and formless void (Genesis 1:1). ~ *Feeding Crowd confirms Jesus as the Savour of life. CF early Humanity*

We all have within us this capacity for creativity as a means of expressing ourselves, our thoughts and our feelings, some more so than others. Nevertheless, it does not matter whether we are great artists or inventors or, as with the majority, ordinary cooks or carpenters, singers or painters, nor whether our creativity is in our homes or elsewhere. What is important is that we can often achieve something that can be appreciated by those to whom we offer the results of our creativity.

Discussion

As a group, discuss how any creative activity has been beneficial to yourselves or others. *Think about creation.*

LIFE *5~1 P*

It can be very good for us to express our creativity. Too often our response to encouragement to be creative is that we are not good enough, or that others are so much better. We may not even see our humble efforts in the kitchen, workshop or garden as being 'creative'. Yet very often they are just that, using our hands to express our thoughts and feelings to produce an artistic or practical outcome for the enjoyment (or amusement!) of others as well as ourselves.

Spend a few minutes thinking about your own creative outlets. The following questions may be helpful as you do so:

Do you allow yourself enough time for creative activity?

What gives you pleasure through creativity?

Does it help you to pray as you create?

Can you see how your acts of creativity may be, in themselves, a form of prayer?

Response
Are there people whom you need to pray for or thank for teaching or encouraging you in your creativity? Do you need to look more closely at what your creative self needs? Share one thing you have learned about yourself or others from the 'Life' section, then discuss together the insights you have shared. 15-20

Worship time.

MEDITATION 19-20

Jesus, the Creator
Ours is a spoken world
called forth by a word more powerful than time itself,
gathered from the grains of the cosmos
and spun together by the power of the Creator.
The vision that brought us into being
gives us creativity as it does so.
We can make of it what we will –
good or bad, evil or blessing;
it lies within our own hands.
Deep within us lies the image of God
waiting for expression, patient, to be called forth.
Shall I paint or carve, write or sing
the character, name or likeness of
the One who fashioned me,
who made me stand and face his world?
Or shall I turn instead to look upon
the possibilities stored up in this piece of wood or stone
or lying within this page, waiting to be discovered?
Can I learn to see beyond the limit of
the present within my immediate vision
and gaze upon the realm waiting to be explored?

Praise

Leader: Lord, you made the foundation of the earth.
All: We will sing together.
Leader: You laid the cornerstone of the world.
All: We will sing together.
Leader: You created the morning stars.
All: All the angels shout for joy.

(Based on Job 38:4–7)

Read Hymn - Open Prayers / silence Music?

READINGS FOR THE WEEK

1 Hands that create

Reflection	Day 5 Day 6 Day 7	Genesis 1:1–31; God who creates John 1:1–13; Jesus, the creative word John 8:1–11; Ephesians 2:1–10 Hands that speak. Hands that made us a new creation

2 Hands that care

Preparation ◆ Meeting	Day 1 Day 2 Day 3 Day 4	Luke 15:11–24; The father who cares Luke 10:25–37; The stranger who cares Matthew 9:18–25; The Lord who cares Matthew 19:13–15; Hands that cared for children

PATTERN OF PRAYER

You may like to use this pattern as a basis for your daily prayers during the course.

Praise and thanksgiving
Spend a few moments thinking of the things you want to thank God for, then offer them up to him in praise.

> I give thanks to the Lord because of his
>   righteousness.
> I sing praises to the name of the Lord Most High.
> O Lord, how majestic is your name in all the
>   earth.
>
> *(Based on Psalms 7:17; 8:1)*

Confession
Spend a few moments thinking of things you need to confess, asking for forgiveness.

> Let us return to the Lord,
> For our God is a God of grace.
> Let us return to the Lord

continued

For our God is a God of compassion.
Let us return to the Lord,
For he is abounding in love.

(Based on Joel 2:12–13)

Bible

On each day when you are preparing for the next session, read the Bible passage and spend time reflecting on it, making notes of any feelings you experience.

Or

On each day when you are reflecting on the last session, re-read the key Bible passage for the session and make notes of any new thoughts or feelings you have.

Then

Use the reading for the day, or the meditation for the week to come, and be still before God.

Intercession

Bring to God:
- any people or situations that you feel need his love
- the other members of the group
- your own needs

The Lord's Prayer

Our Father in heaven,
hallowed be your name,
your kingdom come,
your will be done on earth,
as it is in heaven.

Give us today our daily bread.
Forgive us our sins
as we forgive those who sin against us.
Lead us not into temptation
but deliver us from evil.
For the kingdom, the power and the glory are yours
now and forever. Amen.

In closing
Restore me, Lord, and let your face shine upon me that I may
be saved. Amen.

2 HANDS THAT CARE

Aim: To look at the part that caring plays in our lives.

WAY IN

Each of us at some time will have been cared for by someone, or will have found ourselves in the position of care-giver. Spend a few minutes with another member of the group talking about ways in which it is possible to express care for others. Pray about any particular concerns that arise.

Songs to sing
Hark the glad sound! SOF 154, MP 210.
He's got the whole wide world in His hands, MP 225.
Here, O my Lord, MP 230.
I heard the voice of Jesus say, SOF 215, MP 275, TS 206.
Jesus, how lovely You are, SOF 287, MP 361, TS 279.
Love lifted me! MP 450.
Our confidence is in the Lord, SOF 452, TS 417.
Praise, my soul, the King of heaven, SOF 466, MP 560, TS 433.
Safe in the shadow of the Lord, MP 583.
We rest on Thee, SOF 587, MP 735.

Music to listen to
Yo-Yo Ma: '*Gigue from Suite No. 5 in C minor*', from Bach:
The Six Unaccompanied Cello Suites.
Ladysmith Black Mambazo: '*Abantwana Basethempeleni*'
('Children of the Temple') from In Harmony.
Libera: '*Salva Me*', from Libera.

Read Matthew 19:13–15

[13] Then little children were being brought to him in order
that he might lay his hands on them and pray. The disciples spoke sternly to those who brought them; [14] but Jesus
said, 'Let the little children come to me, and do not stop
them; for it is to such as these that the kingdom of heaven
belongs.' [15] And he laid his hands on them and went on his
way.

Throughout his ministry, Jesus expressed his care for others
in a variety of ways. In particular, Matthew, Mark (10:13–16)
and Luke (18:15–17) give an account of people bringing
babies and young children to Jesus. When the disciples
rebuked them, Jesus in turn rebuked the disciples, telling
them to let the children be brought to him.
Why did people bring their young ones to Jesus anyway? It
does not seem that it was for healing; rather, Jesus was obviously someone who commanded their respect and they
wanted their children to receive his blessing through his laying his hands on them. By contrast, Jairus came because his
daughter was ill (Matthew 9:18–19); but here too Jesus
showed his compassion through touch. These parents just
wanted Jesus' touch because they felt this would benefit their
little ones. Their instincts were right.

An important feature of the Christian approach to life is the proper expression of loving concern through the way in which we care for others. Indeed, it is something that many folk around us share. An important aspect of love is giving physical expression to our caring feelings in appropriate ways.

By our prayers and expressions of concern through whatever channels are open to us, we can help to restore the ground that has been lost through activities of the tiny minority who have abused the trust placed in them. This is something which we should all see as an important task in our Christian journey. We and those we trust to teach or care for others, young and old alike, should not allow ourselves to lose our right to show our love, care and concern for others by default.

Discussion

As a group, discuss how someone's caring touch may have been beneficial to you or to someone you know. You may also wish to talk about the problems associated with touching when caring.

LIFE

In an environment that emphasises the value placed on mental and physical toughness, it is all too easy to see caring and compassion as third-rate attributes. In such a highly individualistic environment, some may feel that any move to express feelings through touch is 'an invasion of personal space.' Yet to hold another person's hand or give them a compassionate hug can bring great reassurance and comfort.

Spend a few minutes thinking about those occasions when you have been moved by compassion.

When you have given physical expression to those feelings of compassion for another person, what effect has this had on you and, if you are aware of it, on the other person?

When someone else has expressed physically their feelings of compassion towards you, what effect has this had on your feelings about them?

RESPONSE

As a group, discuss any response to the 'Life' section which has caused you to think about reviewing your feelings about the use of touch in care-giving. Pray together for any issues that have arisen.

MEDITATION

Hands that care
The hand he held was like a feather, slender and frail.
The child's face was calm and pale.
Hers was the rest of one whose life
battles against the belief of others
in the inevitability that death will be victorious
even over one so young.
Yet there will always be times like this
when God will be glorified.
Faith that foresees wholeness

and recognises the image of God in his creation, can awaken
us to new possibilities.
This little one will awake
and vindicate her father's belief that all was not lost.
The hand I hold is like a feather, slender and frail.
As the last breath expires, the face slowly rests and the lines
of years recede.
The shared communion of touch
has enabled this last journey
to be made in companionship
felt through the warmth of another traveller.
The world will consign this body to its grave
but the soul will journey to eternity.
Is this what we envisage?

Praise

Leader: The Lord leads us to the quiet place.
All: We will keep close to our God.
Leader: The Lord restores our souls.
All: We will keep close to our God.
Leader: Your soul will delight in the richest fare.
All: Let us listen that our souls may live.

(Based on Psalm 23)

READINGS FOR THE WEEK

2 Hands that care

Reflection	Day 5	John 21:15–19; Caring despite the cost
	Day 6	1 Timothy 6:17–19; Our responsibility to care
	Day 7	1 Peter 5:1–11; The leader's responsibility to care

3 Hands that heal

Preparation	Day 1	Mark 1:29–34; Healing hands
	Day 2	Mark 1:40–45; The healing touch
	Day 3	Mark 9:14–29; Healing the spirit
◆ Meeting	Day 4	John 9:1–7; An unlikely balm

3 HANDS THAT HEAL

Aim: To look at the ways in which creativity and caring can come together in healing.

WAY IN   10-15 mins

Each of us will have observed the way in which healing can be greatly helped by the skill of a doctor or physiotherapist. Often this skill is exercised by, or expressed in, the use of hands – very directly so, in the case of physiotherapy. Talk with another member of the group about any experience you may have had of this kind of care, whether personally or in relation to someone you care for.

Songs to sing
Draw me closer, Lord, SOF 81, TS 84.
Guide me, O Thou Great Jehovah, SOF 148, MP 201.
Have Thine own way, Lord, SOF 156, MP 212.
I will sing the wondrous story, SOF 278, MP 315.
Lord, it is eventide, MP 434.
Lord, keep my heart tender, SOF 359.
O let the Son of God enfold you, MP 502, TS 392.
On Jordan's bank the Baptist's cry, MP 538.
Praise You, Lord, SOF 472, MP 565.

When to our world the Saviour came, MP 761.

Music to listen to
Yo-Yo Ma: '*Sarabande from Suite No. 1 in G major*', from Bach: The Six Unaccompanied Cello Suites.
Ladysmith Black Mambazo: '*Amazing Grace*' ('Closer my God to Thee') from In Harmony.
Libera: '*Angelis*', from Libera.

Read John 9:1–7   20-30mins

[1] As he walked along, he saw a man blind from birth. [2] His disciples asked him, 'Rabbi, who sinned, this man or his parents, that he was born blind?' [3] Jesus answered, 'Neither this man nor his parents sinned; he was born blind so that God's works might be revealed in him. [4] We must work the works of him who sent me while it is day; night is coming when no one can work. [5] As long as I am in the world, I am the light of the world.' [6] When he had said this, he spat on the ground and made mud with the saliva and spread the mud on the man's eyes, [7] saying to him, 'Go, wash in the pool of Siloam' (which means Sent). Then he went and washed and came back able to see.

Immediate reflection.

In the restoration of the sight of the blind man, Jesus gives us a very practical demonstration of healing. Both the use of soil and saliva to make a paste, and then its application to the blind man's eyes, involved him in getting his hands dirty in a good cause. Many doctors, nurses and surgeons do the same each and every day, and sometimes in very primitive conditions. A war zone or refugee camp often demands imaginative improvisation, infinite care and great dexterity to make up for a lack of materials and facilities.

However, in this instance it seemed that the main obstacle Jesus had to contend with was the viewpoint of his time, which was that illness came about as the result of sin. This attitude tended to burden the sick person and his family with feelings of guilt and blame, besides the actual suffering caused by the illness itself. Jesus' response was to assert – indeed, to demonstrate – that the man's blindness was not the product of sinfulness but, rather, an opportunity for God to work in his life.

People's attitudes seem to make a difference to whether or not healing can come. Jairus showed great determination and faith when he asked Jesus to heal his daughter: 'Come and lay your hands on her, so that she may be made well, and live' (Mark 5:23). However, in his home town, Jesus was able to do little because of the lack of faith shown by the people there, 'except that he laid his hands on a few sick people and cured them' (Mark 6:5). Earlier, at Capernaum, the faith of his friends made all the difference to a paralysed man's quest for healing (Mark 8:22–25).

Discussion

The Christian church in modern times has found the whole question of healing difficult to deal with. There have been claims and counterclaims as to its appropriateness and efficacy. However, many people have experienced substantial healing – or, at least, have felt better in themselves – as the result of the laying on of hands, especially when this has been given in the context of a search for wholeness, or healing of the whole person, as opposed to seeking a cure for just the ailment itself.

As a group, discuss how you approach this issue, either from your own experience, as a result of supporting someone else, or of observing the laying on of hands, for example, in a public service.

LIFE 5-10

Our approach to this aspect of Jesus' ministry can be coloured by good or bad experiences of our own or those of someone we care about. Spend a few minutes thinking about the issues that have emerged so far, then consider the following questions:

How do you view Christian healing? Does it produce a positive or negative response in you? Are you aware of why you feel as you do?

How do you respond to the laying on of hands for healing, as opposed, say, to the laying on of hands in order to bless?

Do you respond positively or negatively to the distinction between seeking wholeness and seeking a cure?

What part should prayer play in these activities?

RESPONSE ~~15~~ -20

As a group, discuss together any fresh insights that have emerged in the 'Life' section. Pray about issues that may have arisen, especially regarding healing prayer.

MEDITATION 20 mins.

Hands that heal
Sometimes the battered mind will close upon itself
to shut out pain it can no longer stand.
Then the way is barred and shuttered against intrusion.
A silent world descends to shroud the memory

in a cloak of darkness which
allows no interruption.
But there is a way,
whether through music,
the words of caring love,
pictures of summer light
or hands that hold and comfort,
to open gently a pathway leading forward.
This moment spent together calls to mind
that time or place which was more special
because it became, for you, the recollection of good things.
It is here that you can go in your mind's eye,
to claim a fresh start
or to rest awhile in respite from the journey.
Let these hands offer you a companion to go with you,
to listen and to stand ready to catch you if you stumble.
Healing may help you to end the journey in company,
to begin anew or just take stock.
Be sure there will be a change – and for the better.

Praise

Leader: The Lord lifts us when we are down.
All: We will exalt His Name.
Leader: The Lord is our salvation.
All: We will exalt His name.
Leader: We will call on the Lord our God.
All: The Lord will be our healer.

(Based on Psalm 30:1–3)

READINGS FOR THE WEEK

3 Hands that heal

Reflection	Day 5	Mark 16:14–20; The healing hands of the disciples
	Day 6	Acts 3:1–10; Peter's healing hand
	Day 7	Acts 28:7–10; Paul's healing hand

4 Hands that serve

Preparation	Day 1	Luke 17:7–10; Responsibility of the servant
	Day 2	Luke 10:38–42; Martha's distractions
	Day 3	John 12:1–8; Mary's service
◆ Meeting	Day 4	John 13:1–17; Washing the disciples' feet

_4_ SERVING HANDS

Aim: To look at how we are, or how we could be, of service to those around us.

WAY IN

Discuss with another member of the group how you feel about being of service to others.

Songs to sing
Brother, let me be your servant, SOF 54.
I just want to praise You, SOF 218, MP 276, TS 208.
I love You, O Lord, You alone, MP 286.
In Christ there is no east or west, MP 329.
Meekness and majesty, SOF 390, MP 465, TS 353.
My song is love unknown, SOF 400, MP 478.
O Lord, most Holy God, SOF 424, MP 505.
There is a name I love to hear, SOF 543, MP 672.
What a friend we have in Jesus, SOF 593, MP 746, TS 566.
What kind of love is this, MP 750, TS 568.

Music to listen to
Yo-Yo Ma: 'Sarabande from Suite No. 4 in E flat major', from Bach: The Six Unaccompanied Cello Suites.

Ladysmith Black Mambazo: *'Baba Wethu Singenile'* ('Our Father we are here') from In Harmony.
Libera: *'Libera'*, from Libera.

Read John 13:1–17

20-30min

[1] Now before the festival of the Passover, Jesus knew that his hour had come to depart from this world and go to the Father. Having loved his own who were in the world, he loved them to the end. [2] The devil had already put it into the heart of Judas son of Simon Iscariot to betray him. And during supper [3] Jesus, knowing that the Father had given all things into his hands, and that he had come from God and was going to God, [4] got up from the table, took off his outer robe, and tied a towel around himself. [5] Then he poured water into a basin and began to wash the disciples' feet and to wipe them with the towel that was tied around him. [6] He came to Simon Peter, who said to him, 'Lord, are you going to wash my feet?' [7] Jesus answered, 'You do not know now what I am doing, but later you will understand.' [8] Peter said to him, 'You will never wash my feet.' Jesus answered, 'Unless I wash you, you have no share with me.' [9] Simon Peter said to him, 'Lord, not my feet only but also my hands and my head!' [10] Jesus said to him, 'One who has bathed does not need to wash, except for the feet, but is entirely clean. And you are clean, though not all of you.' [11] For he knew who was to betray him; for this reason he said, 'Not all of you are clean.'
[12] After he had washed their feet, had put on his robe, and had returned to the table, he said to them, 'Do you know what I have done to you? [13] You call me Teacher and Lord – and you are right, for that is what I am. [14] So if I, your Lord and Teacher, have washed your feet, you also ought

to wash one another's feet. [15] For I have set you an example, that you also should do as I have done to you. [16] Very truly, I tell you, servants are not greater than their master, nor are messengers greater than the one who sent them. [17] If you know these things, you are blessed if you do them...'

When Jesus washed the disciples' feet, he presented them with a problem. The idea of someone whom they regarded as their Master becoming their servant troubled some disciples, notably Peter. It is indeed often unnerving to find someone we know in one role filling another, especially if we see it as a less important one.

Then there is the difficulty this whole idea of service can give us. There was a time when 'going into service' was a very honourable thing to do. It proved that someone had been properly brought up, could be trusted and knew how to conduct themselves. In recent times, the idea of service has become far less respected. The word 'servant' is now almost derogatory.

By contrast, Jesus tells us just what he means by being of service: 'whoever wishes to be great among you must be your servant, and whoever wishes to be first among you must be your slave' (Matthew 20:26–27). He makes it clear that those who aspire to the highest positions must look on themselves as the servants of all; otherwise they will not fulfill the responsibilities of leadership properly. It is a hard lesson, and sometimes it seems that not many have learned it. Being a servant is frequently regarded as failure, whereas being at the top and served by all is viewed as success. The danger of such an attitude is that it can lead to arrogance and a certain deafness to points of view at odds with our own. This is in stark contrast to the attitude of Paul, for example, who saw himself as just a servant to whom God had given a job (1 Corinthians 3:5–9).

Discussion

We will all, at some time or another, have experienced good service and bad. We may also have seen those on the receiving end of service behaving ungraciously. Today, for example, thanking someone for good service is not fashionable. As a group, exchange views on the importance of respect for those who provide service and those who receive it.

LIFE

Are you a good servant? Would you be happy to 'wash another's feet', as it were? Spend a few minutes reflecting on the ways in which you are of service to others and they to you. Think about situations where you have either to give instructions to others or to carry them out, maybe at work, maybe outside of work or in the home. Perhaps you provide a service by helping someone out (for example, by child-minding).

How does it feel to be told what to do?

How difficult or easy is it to offer to do something rather than wait to be asked to do it?

How important is the manner in which a request to do something is made, or in which a task is carried out?

How difficult or easy is it to give instructions respectfully?

RESPONSE

As a group, talk about any fresh insights gained during the 'Life' section.

Lad/Smith -12

Music:- Bach ~ 10

MEDITATION

Serving hands

She was always busy, cooking, cleaning, tidying, making and mending. Her kitchen was the centre of a world of mysterious aromas which turned miraculously into delicious treats.

It was also a source of wisdom born of long years of giving as wife and mother, friend and housekeeper. Her insights came from patience in listening, pondering and storing, and from humility before her God. Her words were sparingly given but full of thoughtfulness.

She was known to everyone by her surname. Just one name to describe a lifetime's service. But, when she retired, she left a space the size of a dictionary. She had spent her time giving to others but her heart was in the hands of her God to whom she offered her life each day.

Praise

Leader: Lord, you choose those who will serve you.

All: Help us to do your will.

Leader: Lord, you prune for fruitfulness.

All: Help us do your will.

Leader: Lord, you command us to be loving servants.

All: Through your grace we will bear fruit that will last.

(Based on John 15:1–17)

7 Brother, Sister.

- Open prayer.
  - Service to us)
  - Help to serve others.

READINGS FOR THE WEEK

4 Hands that serve

Reflection	Day 5	Matthew 4:1–11; The service of angels
	Day 6	John 19:38–42; The service of friends
	Day 7	Matthew 25:14–30; The quality of service

5 Crucified hands

Preparation	Day 1	Psalm 51:6–19; True sacrifice
	Day 2	Mark 8:31–38; Personal sacrifice
	Day 3	Isaiah 53:1–12; God's perfect sacrifice
◆ Meeting	Day 4	Matthew 27:32–37; Carrying the cross

5 CRUCIFIED HANDS

Aim: To look at the place of sacrifice in our lives.

WAY IN

Discuss with another member of the group a sacrifice by another person which has made a difference in your life.

Songs to sing

Broken for me, broken for you, SOF 53, MP 66, TS 58.

Come and see, SOF 67, MP 85, TS 70.

From heaven you came, SOF 120, MP 162, TS 114.

His hands were pierced, MP 232.

Jesus, stand among us, SOF 303, MP 381.

Just as I am, SOF 316, MP 396, TS 306.

See him come (his body was broken), SOF 490.

See him on the cross of shame, MP 592.

When I survey the wondrous cross, SOF 596, MP 755, TS 572.

You laid aside your majesty, SOF 633, MP 795, TS 601.

Music to listen to

Yo-Yo Ma: '*Sarabande from Suite No. 5 in C minor*', from Bach: The Six Unaccompanied Cello Suites.

Ladysmith Black Mambazo: '*Vuka Jonah Sithandazae*' ('Wake

up Jonah let us pray') from In Harmony.
Libera: '*Lux Aeterna*', from Libera.

Read Matthew 27:32–37; John 20:24–29

[32] As they went out, they came upon a man from Cyrene named Simon; they compelled this man to carry [Jesus'] cross. [33] And when they came to a place called Golgotha (which means Place of a Skull), [34] they offered [Jesus] wine to drink, mixed with gall; but when he tasted it, he would not drink it. [35] And when they had crucified him, they divided his clothes among themselves by casting lots; [36] then they sat down there and kept watch over him. Over his head they put the charge against him, which read, 'This is Jesus, the King of the Jews.'

[24] But Thomas (who was called the Twin), one of the twelve, was not with them when Jesus came. [25] So the other disciples told him, 'We have seen the Lord.' But he said to them, 'Unless I see the mark of the nails in his hands, and put my finger in the mark of the nails and my hand in his side, I will not believe.'
[26] A week later his disciples were again in the house, and Thomas was with them. Although the doors were shut, Jesus came and stood among them and said, 'Peace be with you.' [27] Then he said to Thomas, 'Put your finger here and see my hands. Reach out your hand and put it in my side. Do not doubt but believe.' [28] Thomas answered him, 'My Lord and my God!' [29] Jesus said to him, 'Have you believed because you have seen me? Blessed are those who have not seen and yet have come to believe.'

In a sense the different roles in which we see the hands of Jesus play a part come together on the cross. Jesus the servant who loved enough to wash the disciples' feet also loves enough to 'lay down his life for his friends'. We are his friends if we do as he commands (John 15:13–14).

In dying for us, Jesus reconciles – that is to say, heals – the rift between God and ourselves through the cross (Colossians 1:21–23). God cared enough for us to allow this to happen, and Jesus is the embodiment of the God who cares – Jesus, the Word of God, who was present at the beginning of the world, through whom God acted and then created our opportunity for salvation. So it is that when Jesus says to Thomas, 'See my hands', he is showing him the physical summation of all his work on this earth. Jesus is the resurrected Lord whose work in time is nearing its completion in eternity through his return to heaven. His body bears the marks to prove it.

The work that Jesus started continues today. Around the world, in refugee camps, in areas of natural disaster, or in places of poverty and disease, there are still people motivated to sacrifice themselves for others. Sometimes this is for a short time only; for others it is a lifetime's work. And there are those who make sacrifices to support them. Whichever role we take, however small, we can all play a part (Luke 21:1–4).

Discussion
Discuss, as a group, your reaction to the story of Thomas. Would you have said what Thomas said? How would you have reacted when shown Jesus' hands?

LIFE

Very few of us are called upon to lay down our lives for our friends. In times of war or crisis, great heroism can be displayed; but otherwise, the journey towards the ultimate sacrifice is rare. Yet many smaller but nonetheless important sacrifices are made each day as we help others around us. Spend a few minutes reflecting on the place of sacrifice in your life. The following questions may help you to do so:

Are there things that you do for others which mean your putting to one side your own interests?

Do you pray over your decisions in this area, either that your actions will be imbued with God's love, or that he will help you to pull through (or both)?

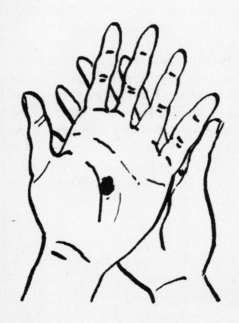

Can you see any beneficial effect as a result of the sacrifices that you or others have made?

How do you feel about the sacrifices you have made for others or that they have made for you?

RESPONSE

As a group, discuss any discoveries made by group members during the 'Life' section.

MEDITATION

Crucified hands

When I look back on the last few days, when I hold up my hands and see the holes left by the nails, I cannot help but wonder. These hands made a lot of things, they comforted many people, they healed others through the power of my Father working in me. I think of the work done at home for my mother, of the feet I washed for the disciples, and I ponder the short time it took to render me powerless to do any of these things, and I wonder at it. Why do some people find it easier to destroy than to create, to harm rather than offer comfort, to injure or cause pain than to heal? Some wanted me to become a king, to organise a revolution. When I refused, I became the token victim of their frustration. Others wanted to stop my work because, as they saw it, I threatened their privileges. Far easier to dispose of me than to change their hearts and minds. My Father had other plans. I am alive and my hands will heal, although I will always bear the scars.

However, healing will continue as will the other things my disciples do in my name. Some will always find destruction attractive, but my words will live forever.

Praise

Leader: Lord, you want us to renew our minds.
All: Let the Holy Spirit renew us.
Leader: Lord, you will accept our offering of ourselves.
All: Let the Holy Spirit renew us.
Leader: Lord, your will is good, pleasing and perfect.
All: We thank you for your mercy towards us.

(Based on Romans 12:1–2)

READINGS FOR THE WEEK

5 Crucified hands

Reflection	Day 5	John 10:22–30; Following the Shepherd
	Day 6	Ephesians 4:17 – 5:1; Fragrant offering
	Day 7	1 Peter 2:4–10; Spiritual sacrifice

6 Hands that bless

Preparation	Day 1	Luke 6:27–36; Blessing those who curse
	Day 2	John 2:1–11; Creative blessing
	Day 3	Galatians 3:6–14; Promise of the Spirit
◆ Meeting	Day 4	Luke 24:13–35; Blessing from the Bread of Life

6 HANDS THAT BLESS

Aim: To look at some of the things Jesus asks his followers to do.

WAY IN

Talk with another member of the group about one thing that you regard as important to you as a follower of Jesus Christ.

Songs to sing
Abide with me, SOF 2, MP 4, TS 2.
I cannot count Your blessings, Lord, MP 265.
Led like a lamb to the slaughter, SOF 322, MP 402, TS 312.
Let us break bread together, SOF 330, MP 414.
Lord, how majestic You are SOF 355.
Lord Jesus Christ, SOF 357, MP 435.
Take, eat, this is my body, SOF 518, MP 622.
We break this bread, SOF 573, MP 721.
We come as guests invited, MP 723.
When I feel the touch, SOF 594, MP 753, TS 570.

Music to listen to
Yo-Yo Ma: 'Prelude from Suite No. 1 in G major', from Bach: The 6 Unaccompanied Cello Suites.

Ladysmith Black Mambazo: '*Oh Happy Day*' from In Harmony.
Libera: '*Sancta*', from Libera.

Read Luke 24:13–32

[13] Now on that same day two of [Jesus' disciples] were going to a village called Emmaus, about seven miles from Jerusalem, [14] and talking with each other about all these things that had happened. [15] While they were talking and discussing, Jesus himself came near and went with them, [16] but their eyes were kept from recognizing him. [17] And he said to them, 'What are you discussing with each other while you walk along?' They stood still, looking sad. [18] Then one of them, whose name was Cleopas, answered him, 'Are you the only stranger in Jerusalem who does not know the things that have taken place there in these days?' [19] He asked them, 'What things?' They replied, 'The things about Jesus of Nazareth, who was a prophet mighty in deed and word before God and all the people, [20] and how our chief priests and leaders handed him over to be condemned to death and crucified him. [21] But we had hoped that he was the one to redeem Israel. Yes, and besides all this, it is now the third day since these things took place. [22] Moreover, some women of our group astounded us. They were at the tomb early this morning, [23] and when they did not find his body there, they came back and told us that they had indeed seen a vision of angels who said that he was alive. [24] Some of those who were with us went to the tomb and found it just as the women had said; but they did not see him.' [25] Then he said to them, 'Oh, how foolish you are, and how slow of heart to believe all that the prophets have declared! [26] Was it not necessary that the Messiah should suffer these things

and then enter into his glory?' ^{27} Then beginning with Moses and all the prophets, he interpreted to them the things about himself in all the scriptures.

^{28} As they came near the village to which they were going, he walked ahead as if he were going on. ^{29} But they urged him strongly, saying, 'Stay with us, because it is almost evening and the day is now nearly over.' So he went in to stay with them. ^{30} When he was at the table with them, he took bread, blessed and broke it, and gave it to them. ^{31} Then their eyes were opened, and they recognized him; and he vanished from their sight. ^{32} They said to each other, 'Were not our hearts burning within us while he was talking to us on the road, while he was opening the scriptures to us?'

At the Last Supper (Luke 22:7–23) Jesus made it clear that the end of his earthly life was near and that those who wanted to kill him would soon have their way – indeed, one of his own followers would betray him. Then he shared himself with his disciples: he took the bread and the wine, gave thanks for them, then gave them to those closest to him. As he did this, he likened the bread and wine to his own body and blood which would soon be broken and spilt by other hands. He instructed his disciples to remember him by sharing bread and wine in the same way.

Later, on the road to Emmaus, Jesus joined two disciples who were obviously depressed by his crucifixion and puzzled by some of the subsequent reports of his resurrection. These disciples did not recognise him immediately from his physical appearance. It is interesting to think that we too would be unable to recognise Jesus from his physical appearance, because no picture of him was ever made during his lifetime, nor is there a description of him in the Gospels. Nevertheless, Jesus' companions recognised him the moment he broke bread and gave it to them. His hands, his gestures and the way he served them were all a sufficient, powerful and revealing witness to the reality of his presence.

This is a reminder to us of his instruction that if we love him we will obey his commandments (John 15:9–10). We can confirm that obedience is at the heart of our love for Jesus when we, in our turn, offer our hands to receive the bread and wine given to us in his name, and then share with others what we ourselves have received: 'Freely you have received, freely give' (Matthew 10:8b, NIV).

MEDITATION

Hands that bless

When we come in peace and bring hope as our companion, our fists are not clenched, we need no threats or weapons. Love cannot be held in closed hands, nor is hope carried by a baseball bat or bullet. The hand that hurls the stone or rock throws hope away with anger and unreason. On the ground, alongside the stricken victim, lies our claim to have risen above the barbaric.

Love is not a cause but a way of living; it is we who choose the actions for our hands. When we clench a fist to strike, or grasp a weapon, we drive a nail through the palm of hope. Love for our neighbour is the first victim of war, on whose battlefield our hope of humanity lies trampled underfoot.

When I offer you my love, I do so with my hands open and my palms towards you. If you ask for my blessing, I will give it to you unconditionally; but you must act to claim it for yourself by being a blessing to others.

LIFE

Spend some time reflecting on the means of remembrance that Jesus left for us. The same Eucharist can, after all, mean many different things to its participants, depending largely on what they bring to it by way of burdens and expectations. It also draws us in to one of the most intimate moments of Jesus' life.

Write your own prayer, meditation or reflection on the meaning for you of the Last Supper and the commandment to 'do this in remembrance of me'.

Note to leaders: You may wish to consider using some or all of these prayers as part of the response to this section.

RESPONSE — Some Symbolic Action.

An Agape or service of communion could be held before or after the session at which some of these prayers, etc could be used.

Praise

Leader: Lord, take away our pride.
All: Help us to be a blessing to those we meet.
Leader: May we repay evil with good.
All: Help us to be a blessing to those we meet.
Leader: When we face scorn and persecution
All: May we bless, not curse.

(Based on Romans 12:14–20)

READINGS FOR THE WEEK

6 Hands that bless

Reflection	Day 5	Matthew 25:31–46; Do what is right
	Day 6	Romans 12:9–21; Bless and do not curse
	Day 7	Luke 24:36–53; Go out with blessing

Other Resources from Scripture Union

Closer to God
Reading the Bible in the power of the Holy Spirit
ISSN 1362-914X, £2.65 per quarter

Quarterly notes with a creative and reflective approach and emphasising renewal. There is a Bible reading with notes for each day of the week, together with 'going deeper' meditations, special features and theme weeks.

Sitting at the Feet of Jesus
Stephen and Jacalyn Eyre
ISBN 1 85999 020 7, £3.50

This Spiritual Encounter Guide on the Sermon on the Mount offers a fresh approach to personal devotion for new or long-time Christians. The aim of these Bible studies is to help readers find intimacy with God. The book contains one month's Bible reading material.

Journey into the Bible
John Drane
ISBN 1 85999 409 1, £4.99

In his usual thought-provoking and accessible style John Drane gives a stimulating introduction to many of the issues raised by reading the Bible today. Designed especially for those who are struggling to come to terms with the Bible.

Light from a Dark Star
Where's God when my world falls apart?
Wayne Kirkland
ISBN 1 85999 515 2, £4.99

It's the big question that won't go away. Why does God allow suffering? There are no simple answers in this book. No attempts to shrug off the serious challenges to faith which the question raises. Rather it engages compassionately with the sufferings of real people, grappling with slippery issues, in a discovery of some intriguing perspectives.

Knowing God's Ways
A user's guide to the Old Testament
Patton Taylor
ISBN 1 85999 349 4, £6.99

Do you find the Old Testament difficult to get into? If you've been looking for some help in making sense of it all, then this book by a professor at Union Theological College in Belfast is what you've been looking for! His accessible, user-friendly approach will help you gain a clear overview of the Old Testament, understand different genres, and apply biblical teaching to today's world.

Dangerous Praying
Inspirational ideas for individuals and groups
David Spriggs
ISBN 1 85999 335 4, £6.99

Drawing on Paul's letter to the Ephesians, this creative book challenges us to be bold when we pray, both in what we pray for and how we pray. David Spriggs presents us with 101 practical ideas and strategies to help us develop a courageous prayer life, whether in a group or individually.

Through the Bible in a Year
A spiritual journal
Dennis Lennon
ISBN 1 85999 196 3, £9.99

A new syllabus' constructed around eleven themes, gives an overarching picture of the whole Bible story. There is space for the reader to keep a written record of their spiritual journey.

Ready to Grow
Practical steps to knowing God better
Alan Harkness
ISBN 0 949720 71 2, £5.99

An attractive and practical book to encourage believers to make time with God a regular part of their lives. Includes chapters on preparation, getting started, the practicalities, sharing what you have learned, and different methods of combining Bible reading and prayer.

Faith and Common Sense
Living boldly, choosing wisely
David Dewey
ISBN 1 85999 302 8, £4.99

This unusual book explores how we can live riskily yet sensibly. Drawing on the lives of key Bible characters like Peter, the author first lays a solid biblical and theological foundation for achieving a balance. Then follows a practical look at areas in our lives where a need for that balance is vital – healing, the gifts of the Spirit, work, money, failure and guidance.

The Bible Unwrapped
Developing your Bible skills
David Dewey
ISBN 1 85999 533 0, £5.99

Is the Bible something of a closed book to you? Here you'll find help in finding your way around the Bible, and in grasping the big picture of the Bible's message. You'll also learn to appreciate the different types of literature in the Bible and be introduced to eight different approaches to Bible study. Clear and accurate charts and diagrams and a helpful glossary add value.

How to read the Bible for all its worth
Gordon Fee and Douglas Stuart
ISBN 1 86201 974 5, £7.50

This contemporary classic deals in considerable detail with the principles we need to adopt in studying different biblical genres. The authors, both professors in their respective fields of Old Testament and New Testament, explain clearly and carefully the principles underlying responsible biblical interpreatation and application to the contemporary world. There's no other book as good in its field!

Thank God it's Monday
Ministry in the workplace
Mark Greene
ISBN: 1 85999 503 9, £4.99

Fun, fast, and full of stories, this highly practical book looks at how we can make the most of our time at work, helping us to see our jobs, our co-workers and our bosses the way God does. The third edition of this highly influential classic features an updated resource section and a new chapter on integrating life and work, helping us see how our work life, as well as our weekend life, can be lived fruitfully for God.